GRACEFUL GROWTH

LEARNING LESSONS FROM RAISING CHILDREN

Whispers of Wisdom - 20 Truths Your Children Want You to Hear

Copyright © 2023 by Graceful Growth

All rights reserved. No part of this publication may be reproduced, stored or transmitted in any form or by any means, electronic, mechanical, photocopying, recording, scanning, or otherwise without written permission from the publisher. It is illegal to copy this book, post it to a website, or distribute it by any other means without permission.

Graceful Growth asserts the moral right to be identified as the author of this work.

Graceful Growth has no responsibility for the persistence or accuracy of URLs for external or third-party Internet Websites referred to in this publication and does not guarantee that any content on such Websites is, or will remain, accurate or appropriate.

Designations used by companies to distinguish their products are often claimed as trademarks. All brand names and product names used in this book and on its cover are trade names, service marks, trademarks and registered trademarks of their respective owners. The publishers and the book are not associated with any product or vendor mentioned in this book. None of the companies referenced within the book have endorsed the book.

First edition

This book was professionally typeset on Reedsy. Find out more at reedsy.com

Contents

Foreword		v
1	Introduction	1
2	Lesson 1: "Don't Spoil Me"	4
3	Lesson 2: "Do Not Be Afraid to Be Strict and Strong"	6
4	Lesson 3: "Don't Let Me Create Bad Habits"	9
5	Lesson 4: "Don't Treat Me Younger than I Actually Am"	11
6	Lesson 5: "Don't Scold Me, Punish Me, or Reprimand Me in..."	14
7	Lesson 6: "Don't Force on Me That My Mistakes Are Mortal..."	16
8	Lesson 7: "Don't Be Too Mad When I Say "I Hate You""	18
9	Lesson 8: "Do Not Protect Me from All the Consequences of My..."	20
10	Lesson 9: "Don't Pay Excessive Attention to My Minor..."	22
11	Lesson 10: "Don't Scold Me"	25
12	Lesson 11: "Don't Make Hasty Promises"	27
13	Lesson 12: "Remember That I Can't Always Express Myself..."	30
14	Lesson 13: "Don't Try My Honesty Too Much"	33
15	Lesson 14: "Don't Be Inconsistent"	36
16	Lesson 15: "Don't Tell Me You Don't Like Me When I Make..."	39
17	Lesson 16: "Don't Say My Worries and Fear Are Nonsense"	42

18	Lesson 17: "Don't Try to Tell Me That You Are Perfect and...	45
19	Lesson 18: "Never Think That It Is Below Your Dignity to...	48
20	Lesson 19: "Don't Forget How Fast I'm Growing Up"	51
21	Lesson 20: "Don't Forget That I Can't Grow Up Well Without...	54
22	PARENTING INSIGHTS: KITCHEN WALL SUMMARY	57
23	Conclusion	60
24	THANK YOU!	63

Foreword

ANNOUNCING....Wish you could unlock the secrets to masterful parenting? You can and you will with this swift and straightforward guide—a must-have for every dedicated parent looking to thrive in their role!"

This book is a treasure trove of insights, packaged in an easy-to-digest format with plenty of wisdom revealed by children and learning along the way. Here's what you'll discover inside:

- **Unspoken Insights:** Tap into the often-overlooked wisdom of children with 20 powerful lessons on parenting.
- **Engaging Exchanges:** Enjoy a book that's as entertaining as it is wise, blending examples with practical advice.
- **Timeless Parenting Pearls**: Whether you're a new parent or have been in the trenches, these truths are timeless.
- **Conversation Starters**: Each lesson is a gateway to deeper connection and understanding with your child.
- **A Journey of Growth**: Embark on a narrative that celebrates the growth of both parent and child, filled with stories that resonate and enlighten.

This book prepares you to engage with your child's world in new ways, laugh, and learn. "Learning Lessons from Raising Children" is not just a book; it's an invitation to enrich your parenting with love, humor, self-indulgence, and the genuine voices of children.

1

Introduction

"Unlock the secrets to masterful parenting with this swift and simple guide—a must-have for every dedicated parent looking to thrive in their role!"

W elcome to the pages of a journey unlike any other—a journey into the heart of a child's world as they see it. As you turn these pages, you are invited to kneel down and look into a child's vast, wondering eyes of a child. You'll hear the unspoken words and feel the unexpressed emotions often lost in adulthood's busy hum.

This book isn't just a collection of messages; it's a mosaic of heartfelt needs and silent pleas for understanding, empathy, and genuine connection. Each lesson unfolds a message, a vital piece of advice that children yearn for their parents to grasp, not with their minds but with their hearts.

Through a Child's Eyes - Understanding Growth and Love

Growing up, I often felt like a whisper lost in the clamor of the world around me—a world that seemed to spin without noticing my struggles or hearing my voice. It was a silent battle, feeling misunderstood, unheard, and overlooked. This shadow of my childhood became the blueprint of my resolve when I had my own children. I vowed to be the sanctuary for them that I yearned for in my younger years. With every fiber of my being, I strived to be present, to listen genuinely, and to acknowledge their feelings with the gravity and sensitivity they deserved. I poured the lessons of my own solitude into being there for them, crafting a family tapestry woven with threads of empathy, understanding, and the steadfast promise that I would always hear them. My children's voices became the music I danced to, their joys and sorrows the rhythm of my days as I dedicated myself to nurturing their growth in the warm embrace of being understood.

As the lessons progress, we'll explore the delicate balance between loving generously and spoiling, between guiding firmly and reprimanding harshly. We'll understand the importance of nurturing resilience while providing a safe harbor of support. This is a tale of how small moments shape our identities, how gentle guidance fosters our strengths, and how recognizing our tiny yet significant fears and worries solidifies the trust in our relationships.

By embracing the essence of these twenty messages, parents, guardians, and caregivers are embarking on a transformative experience. This book encourages you to listen to both the laughter and the silence, bold words and the quiet sighs. Here, we speak the language of love that doesn't need loud words but thrives on gentle understanding.

So, as you begin this expedition, remember that you are not just reading a book; you are unlocking the world as perceived by the little ones who hold our hands for a while but our hearts forever. Let their voices guide you through a narrative that promises to enrich the parent-child bond with every word and every message. Welcome to a child's heart. Welcome to our shared journey of

INTRODUCTION

growing, learning, and loving.

LET'S BEGIN...
WHISPERS OF WISDOM - 20 Truths Your Children Want You to Hear

2

Lesson 1: "Don't Spoil Me"

- Explore the balance between giving love and material possessions.
- Discuss the long-term effects of overindulgence.

The Perils of Overindulgence: A Child's Insight on Being Spoiled

I know it feels good to give me everything I want, but when you do, it's hard for me to understand my own limits. Love isn't just about the toys and treats you buy; it's in the hugs, the time spent together, and the lessons taught. If I get all I ask for, I might never learn to appreciate the value of things or the effort it takes to earn them. I might grow up feeling entitled, expecting the world to hand me everything without working for it. Overindulgence might seem like love, but it can set me up for struggles with dissatisfaction and the inability to cope with 'no.' It's okay to say no sometimes; it teaches me that life has ups and downs, and that's all right. Love me, teach me, but let me earn and learn, too, so I grow up knowing love's actual value beyond just material gifts.

LESSON 1: "DON'T SPOIL ME"

Example:

Imagine a child named Alex, whose parents gave him everything he pointed out at the latest video games, a high-end smartphone, and even a mini ATV. To his parents, these gifts were tokens of love, a way to ensure he felt happy and lacked for nothing. However, as Alex grew, so did his expectations. He wanted the new tablet model that had been on the market for just a month. His parents hesitated but eventually gave in, not wanting to see him upset.

Over time, Alex struggled to find joy in simple pleasures. He threw tantrums when denied anything, felt little gratitude, and his friendships suffered because he couldn't relate to peers who didn't have as much. He gave up quickly in school, accustomed to life's rewards with minimal effort. His parents realized that in their attempt to provide a life of abundance, they had denied him the crucial understanding of effort, gratitude, and resilience.

They started small to recalibrate, encouraging Alex to save allowance for non-essential desires and to donate old toys to those in need. They spent more time on activities that didn't involve spending, like family game nights and volunteering. Through these steps, Alex began to understand the non-materialistic aspects of love and the satisfaction of earning and giving, which are far more valuable life lessons.

3

Lesson 2: "Do Not Be Afraid to Be Strict and Strong"

- The importance of setting boundaries for a sense of security.
- How discipline teaches responsibility.

The Strength in Boundaries: A Child's Perspective on Discipline

When you're firm with me, it tells me where the lines are drawn, and within those lines, I find a surprising sense of freedom. Your strength in setting clear boundaries doesn't scare me; it makes me feel safe. It's like having walls on a bridge—I can run and play, knowing I won't fall off. This discipline is more than rules; it teaches me about responsibility and shows me that my actions have consequences. When you stand firm and don't waver, even when I test the limits, you're helping me learn to trust in structure and predictability. It's okay to be strict if it's also fair because then I learn to trust the rules and myself to navigate within them. It's a balance, isn't it? Your strength becomes my security, and from there, I learn to be strong and responsible, too. In

LESSON 2: "DO NOT BE AFRAID TO BE STRICT AND STRONG"

this guidance, I see the framework of respect for both myself and others. Your consistency is a template for the integrity I hope to embody as I grow.

Example:

Imagine a scenario where a child plays at a playground with a clear set of rules: no pushing, take turns on the slides, and stay within the designated play area. The child's caregiver ensures that the child understands these rules and the reasons behind them - safety and fairness.

One day, the child starts to push others to get to the slide first. The caregiver steps in immediately, not with anger, but with firmness, reminding the child of the rules and the importance of taking turns. Instead of being allowed to continue playing, the child is taken aside momentarily to discuss why pushing is unacceptable. The child is then given another chance to play, but with the understanding that if they try again, there will be a consequence, such as leaving the playground for the day.

This firm but fair approach teaches the child that their actions have consequences. It provides a clear boundary that, when crossed, results in a predictable and understood outcome. By being consistent with these boundaries and enforcing rules, the caregiver is teaching the child to respect others, understand the importance of safety, and take responsibility for their actions.

This type of discipline is not about punishment but about guiding the child to know why boundaries exist and to feel secure within them. It's about developing a sense of responsibility that will help the child navigate more complex situations as they grow. The child learns to trust the caregiver as a source of safety and guidance, which in turn helps them develop self-discipline and a sense of integrity that will serve them throughout their life.

4

Lesson 3: "Don't Let Me Create Bad Habits"

- Role of parents in shaping healthy habits.
- Consequences of unchecked bad habits.

Guardians of Good Habits: The Role of Parents

As a kid, I look to you to guide me in forming habits that will shape my future. If I start to develop bad ones, it's not just a phase—it's a plea for your guidance. When you let bad habits slide, they can root deeply, becoming tough to weed out as I grow. These habits could range from poor eating to shirking responsibilities or giving up too quickly. Your role is pivotal; you set the boundaries and show me the rewards of good discipline. If you overlook my unhealthy patterns, they might become ingrained, leading to struggles with self-discipline and self-care later on. It's like planting seeds; nurture the good ones, and I'll grow strong and healthy. Let the weeds take hold, and I'll work much harder to flourish. Guide me with patience and consistency and help me create a foundation of positive habits to support me for a lifetime.

Example:

Consider a child who has started to spend an excessive amount of time playing video games, often at the expense of homework and outdoor playtime. Initially, it seems like a harmless way to unwind, but as time goes on, the child neglects school assignments and becomes less physically active.

The parents notice this emerging pattern and decide to step in. They sit down with the child to discuss the importance of balance and set new guidelines: video games are allowed after homework is completed and some form of physical activity is undertaken. They help the child create a daily schedule that includes time for study, play, and rest.

The parents also engage in activities with the child, perhaps playing a short game together or going for a family bike ride, reinforcing these habits through shared experiences. They praise the child for following the new routine and occasionally check on the homework progress before gaming begins.

By doing so, the parents are helping the child to break the emerging lousy habit of procrastination and replace it with healthier habits like time management and prioritizing responsibilities. The consistent enforcement of these new rules helps the child to understand the consequences of their actions and the long-term benefits of good habits. This approach not only addresses the immediate problem but equips the child with the discipline and self-regulation skills that will benefit them throughout their life.

5

Lesson 4: "Don't Treat Me Younger than I Actually Am"

- Respect my growth; seeing me as younger can damage my self-worth.
- Encourage me to step into each new chapter of my life with confidence.

"**N**urture maturity, foster independence, and honor the childhood journey."

Navigating the complex journey of growing up is challenging enough for children without the added burden of being treated as younger than their actual age. When parents or caregivers underestimate a child's maturity, it can inadvertently send a message that the child is not capable or trusted to act according to their age, which can lead to feelings of frustration or a lack of confidence. As children grow, they strive to find their place in the world, and part of that process is taking on responsibilities that match their developmental stage. Being treated too young can stifle this natural progression, causing them to rebel and act out inappropriately for their age or become overly dependent and less inclined to take on new challenges. Adults must recognize and respect a child's growing independence and capabilities, providing opportunities that foster maturity. This delicate balance encourages children to behave in a way that is congruent with their age, promoting a healthy transition into each new stage of their young lives.

Example:

Imagine a 12-year-old girl named Mia who has always been considered mature for her age. She's responsible, does well in school, and is generally trusted by her parents. However, regarding social events, her parents are hesitant to let her attend gatherings with peers from school, fearing she's not quite ready to handle the social pressures that might come with such independence.

Mia feels ready and has been discussing these events with her friends, who are all going. She understands the potential challenges and wants the opportunity to navigate them with the trust and support of her parents. Mia presents a well-thought-out argument to her parents, outlining how she would handle various situations, and suggests a compromise: she'll check in every hour and has arranged for a friend's older sibling to be a phone call away in case she feels uncomfortable at any time.

Her parents realize that their perception of her as their 'little girl' clashes with the capable young person she's becoming. They decide to allow her to attend, recognizing that she's showing the maturity and judgment necessary for her age. At the event, Mia stays true to her word, checking in with her parents and handling herself with the maturity they hoped

LESSON 4: "DON'T TREAT ME YOUNGER THAN I ACTUALLY AM"

to see. This experience becomes a significant step in her journey toward adolescence, reinforcing her confidence and her parents' trust in her ability to handle more independence.

6

Lesson 5: "Don't Scold Me, Punish Me, or Reprimand Me in Public"

- The importance of privacy in discipline.
- The psychological effects of public reprimands.

"**When You Teach Me, Let It Be Just Between Us.**"

Please talk to me about what I did wrong in private, not in front of others. It really hurts when I get told off where everyone can see. It makes me feel embarrassed and small, and I can't focus on what I did wrong because I'm just thinking about everyone watching me. I can listen better when we're alone and understand why you're upset. I want to learn and do better, but it's hard when I feel ashamed in front of others. I promise I'll learn the lesson, so let's keep those tough talks between us, okay? That way, I can keep my head up and try to fix things without worrying about who else is watching. Creating a private space for these conversations not only helps me listen but also shows me that you respect me and my feelings, which makes me respect and listen to you in return.

LESSON 5: "DON'T SCOLD ME, PUNISH ME, OR REPRIMAND ME IN...

Example:

Consider a scenario where 9-year-old Lucas is at a family gathering, and he gets into a bit of mischief, spilling his drink on the carpet after being repeatedly told to be careful. His mother, feeling the pressure of watching relatives, is about to scold him in front of everyone. However, she pauses, remembering the importance of handling such situations privately.

Instead of reprimanding Lucas then and there, she takes him aside, away from the crowd. In a calm and private setting, she explains why his actions were problematic, discussing the potential consequences and the importance of being careful. Lucas can listen without the added embarrassment of being in the public eye. He understands the lesson, apologizes, and even offers to help clean up the mess.

This approach spares Lucas the humiliation and the stress that would have come with a public scolding. It allows him to maintain his dignity in front of his family and provides a clear, focused opportunity for him to learn from his mistakes. The private conversation also reinforces the bond of trust and respect between Lucas and his mother, showing him that she values his feelings and is constructively committed to his growth.

7

Lesson 6: "Don't Force on Me That My Mistakes Are Mortal Sins"

- Understanding the severity of mistakes and learning from them.
- Encouraging a balanced sense of morality.

"**M**istakes Are for Learning, Not For Shame."
When I mess up, please don't make it seem like I've done the worst thing in the world. It's terrifying to think that a small mistake could be seen as so catastrophic. I understand when I've erred and am eager to make amends, but I must recognize that making mistakes is a natural part of learning. They are the stepping stones to knowledge. If each error is magnified into a colossal blunder, the fear of failure may inhibit me from embracing new experiences or seizing opportunities that foster my development. Let's engage in a constructive dialogue about the nature of my mistake and its significance without casting me as the villain. I'm striving for a balanced moral compass, and I need your support to master the art of resilience in the face of setbacks. Together, let's approach mistakes as lessons to be processed

LESSON 6: "DON'T FORCE ON ME THAT MY MISTAKES ARE MORTAL...

and solved, empowering me to evolve into the finest version of myself. Your guidance inspires me to experiment, learn, and progress without the shadow of unwarranted guilt.

Example:

Imagine a young girl named Madison who accidentally broke a neighbor's window while playing baseball. Upon discovering the incident, her parents could have reacted harshly, making her feel like she had committed an unforgivable act. However, they chose to handle it differently.

They sat Madison down and explained the difference between accidents and deliberate wrongdoing. They discussed the importance of taking responsibility for one's actions, which in this case involved apologizing to the neighbor and finding ways to make amends, such as offering to help pay for the repair. Instead of criticizing her, they focused on the learning aspect of the situation.

By not treating the mistake as a mortal sin, Madison's parents taught her valuable lessons about accountability, honesty, and the importance of making things right when possible. Madison learned that while her actions have consequences, mistakes are not irredeemable and don't define her character. This balanced approach to morality allowed Madison to learn from the incident without carrying the weight of excessive guilt or fear, promoting a healthy understanding of right and wrong.

8

Lesson 7: "Don't Be Too Mad When I Say "I Hate You"

- Navigating emotional outbursts from children.
- Recognizing the underlying feelings and messages.

"**Hear My Feelings, Not Just My Words.**"

When frustration boils over, and I shout, "I hate you," it's not really about hate. It's about the storm of emotions I can't manage yet. I'm still learning to express myself; sometimes, all my feelings get tangled and come out messily. It's like a signal flare, showing I'm overwhelmed or don't understand what's happening. I need your help to figure out what's really going on inside me. Maybe I'm angry, hurt, or just tired. Please see past those hurtful words and recognize the plea for help they really are. Your calmness can be a guide back to my own calm. We can work through the real issue together if you stay patient and don't hold my outburst against me. And remember, even when I say the opposite, I need and love you.

LESSON 7: "DON'T BE TOO MAD WHEN I SAY "I HATE YOU"

Example:

Look at the perspective of a child named Alec who, in a moment of anger during a disagreement about bedtime, yelled, "I hate you!" at his mother. Instead of responding with equal anger or punishment, his mother took a deep breath and calmly acknowledged his feelings.

"Alec, I hear that you're really upset right now," she might say. "It's okay to feel angry, but I know you don't hate me. Let's talk about what's really bothering you once you've calmed down."

Later, when the atmosphere was less charged, Alec's mother revisited the conversation, asking him to explain what upset him. Together, they uncovered that Alec felt left out because his bedtime was earlier than his older sibling's, making him feel younger and less valued. His mother explained the reasons for the different bedtimes but also listened to his feelings, validating his emotions while maintaining the necessary boundaries.

By not reacting harshly to Alec's outburst, his mother showed him that his words, while powerful, would not destabilize their relationship. This approach helped Alec learn to trust that he could express his feelings, even the negative ones, and still be heard and loved. It also taught him that while his words could hurt, they could also be a starting point for a deeper conversation and understanding.

9

Lesson 8: "Do Not Protect Me from All the Consequences of My Actions"

- Teaching accountability and the natural consequences of actions.
- Preparing children for the real world.

"**L**et Me Learn from My Mistakes"

I know it is hard to watch me stumble, but I need to learn that my actions have consequences. Shielding me from them might make things easier in the short term, but in the long run, it doesn't prepare me for the real world in the long run. If I forget my homework, let me face the teacher's disappointment. If I break a rule, I should understand what it means to make amends. It's how I'll learn responsibility and the importance of making good choices. When you step back sometimes, you're not leaving me alone but trusting me to grow. Yes, I'll make mistakes, but I'll also learn how to fix them, and that's a crucial lesson. It builds my confidence and shows me that I'm capable of bouncing back, which is a big part of growing up. Just be there to guide me when I'm genuinely lost and celebrate with me when

LESSON 8: "DO NOT PROTECT ME FROM ALL THE CONSEQUENCES OF MY...

I get it right.

Example:

Imagine a young girl named Sophie who impulsively uses her mother's makeup without permission. She accidentally spills the foundation on the carpet in her enthusiasm, creating a noticeable stain. When her mother discovers the mishap, she resists the urge to clean up the mess immediately.

Instead, she sits down with Sophie and explains the importance of taking responsibility for her actions. Her mother says, "Sophie when we make a mess, we clean it up. Let's figure out how to do this together."

They research and find safe ways to remove makeup from carpets. Sophie spends the afternoon working on the stain, and although it doesn't completely disappear, the process teaches her an invaluable lesson. Her mother praises her for her efforts, but Sophie also has to live with the reminder of the stain in her room, reinforcing the lesson learned.

Sophie's mother understands that protecting her from the consequences of her actions would only serve to delay her understanding of personal responsibility. By allowing Sophie to experience the result of her actions firsthand, her mother ensures that she learns the value of caution and respect for other people's belongings. This kind of experience teaches Sophie that her actions have real-world implications, preparing her for greater responsibilities in the future.

10

Lesson 9: "Don't Pay Excessive Attention to My Minor Injuries"

- Encouraging resilience and self-reliance.
- Differentiating between overprotectiveness and care.

"**Teach Me Resilience, Not Fear.**"

When I scrape my knee or bump my elbow, it's okay not to make a big deal out of it. I look to you to understand how to react; if you're calm, I learn I will be okay. Overreacting might make me feel like the world is full of dangers I can't handle. Of course, I need your hugs and care when I'm hurt, but also show me how to dust myself off and try again. This way, I learned to be resilient and to understand my own strengths. I must know that minor setbacks aren't disasters—they're just part of life. Teach me to treat them as lessons in toughness and healing. This doesn't mean ignoring me when I'm in pain, but instead helping me to gauge what truly needs attention. It's a balance that helps me grow strong in body and mind.

LESSON 9: "DON'T PAY EXCESSIVE ATTENTION TO MY MINOR...

Example:

Nine-year-old Lucas was playing soccer with his friends at the park when he tripped and fell, scraping his knee. It stung, and a bright red abrasion was visible. He looked up to see his dad jogging over, concerned.

His dad, kneeling beside him, smiled quickly and said, "Whoops! That was quite a tumble, huh?" He inspected the knee gently. "Looks like a warrior's badge to me. What do you think?"

Still processing his dad's reaction, Lucas nodded, feeling the sting subside a bit with acknowledgment.

"Let's clean it up when we get home. For now, a little water, and you're good to go," his dad said as he helped Lucas to his feet and poured some water from his bottle over the scrape.

Lucas watched as the water washed away the dirt. His dad handed him a bandana. "Here, pat it dry. You're doing great."

As Lucas patted his knee, his dad said, "You're tough, but remember, it's okay to take a break if you need it."

Lucas shook his head, the hurt knee already becoming a memory. "I want to play some more."

"Alright, then. Go on," his dad encouraged, with a watchful but trusting gaze.

Lucas ran back to the game, the fall already turning into a story to tell, his resilience bolstered by his dad's balanced approach to care and encouragement to overcome small adversities.

11

Lesson 10: "Don't Scold Me"

- Effective communication versus scolding.
- Promoting a dialogue for better understanding.

"**S**peak With Me, Don't Scold Me."

Remember, when you talk with me instead of scolding me, I learn to listen and not just fear. Scolding shuts me down, but conversation opens a path to understanding. If I've done something wrong, help me understand what and why. Let's talk about it so I can learn from my mistakes and not just feel bad about them. When you scold me, I might only learn to avoid getting caught next time, not why it's essential to do the right thing. But when we have a dialogue, you show me respect, and I feel valued. This teaches me to reflect on my actions and their consequences. I learned to think critically and make better choices through calm and constructive conversation. I need your guidance spoken in words that teach, not words that hurt, so our communication builds a bridge, not a wall.

Example:

Twelve-year-old Lisa had just gotten her report card, and the results were unexpected. She had failed her mathematics exam, a subject she had been struggling with. Her mother found the report card on the kitchen table.

Instead of scolding, her mother took a deep breath and sat beside Lisa. "I see the math test didn't go well," she said, her voice even and concerned, "What do you think happened?"

Lisa shrugged, feeling the weight of disappointment, expecting a lecture.

Her mother continued, "I know you've been struggling with math. Do you think there's a way we could work on this together?"

Lisa looked up, surprised by the lack of scolding. "I don't know. Maybe."

"Let's talk about what's been difficult for you," her mother suggested. "And we can come up with a plan. Maybe a tutor or some extra practice. What do you think?"

They spent the next hour discussing Lisa's challenges and fears about the subject. Her mother listened and offered support, turning the failure into a constructive conversation about solutions and strategies.

By the end of the talk, Lisa felt heard and understood, and she had a new sense of determination to improve. She learned a valuable lesson about approaching problems and was grateful for the communication that led to support instead of scolding.

12

Lesson 11: "Don't Make Hasty Promises"

- The importance of trustworthiness and the effects of broken promises.

"**Value Your Promises, They Mean the World to Me.**"

Please think carefully before you make a promise to me. When you commit to something, I take it to heart and wait with hope. If that promise is broken, it's more than just disappointment for me—it shakes my trust. The reliability of your words is the foundation of my sense of security. Every kept promise reinforces my belief in your word and in the world's stability, while every unfulfilled one makes me question your reliability and my expectations from others. I learn about trustworthiness from you, so when you follow through, you're also teaching me to be a person of my word as well. Remember, even the slightest promise holds significant weight in my eyes. Your consistency in keeping promises is crucial; it builds my confidence in you and sets the standard for my integrity.

Example:

Nine-year-old Adam stood eagerly at the window, watching for his father's car. He had been promised a trip to the science museum for weeks, and today was the day it was supposed to happen. His father, a busy lawyer, often found his days unpredictable.

When his father finally arrived, Adam ran to the door when his father finally arrived, but he could tell from his father's expression that the news wasn't good.

"Hey buddy," his father began with a tired smile, "I know we planned to go to the museum today, but something urgent came up at work, and I can't take you."

Adam's face fell. This wasn't the first time Dad broke a promise, and the disappointment stung.

Seeing his son's sadness, his father sat down beside him. "I realize this keeps happening, and I'm truly sorry. I want to make this right. Let's look at my schedule together and pick a day when I'm not swamped so we're sure to go."

Adam nodded, understanding his father's dilemma but also feeling the familiar pang of a promise not kept.

Together, they chose a day two weeks away, and his father put it in his calendar as non-negotiable. "This time, it's a priority," his father assured him. "I promise, and I mean it."

True to his word, they spent the day at the museum two weeks later.

LESSON 11: "DON'T MAKE HASTY PROMISES"

Adam's father had shown him the value of a promise kept, reinforcing trust and teaching Adam the importance of being someone others can rely on.

13

Lesson 12: "Remember That I Can't Always Express Myself Clearly"

- The development of communication skills in children.
- Patience and active listening strategies.

"**Listen to What I Can't Say Out Loud**"

I'm still learning to put my feelings into words, so I might not always say what I mean clearly. It's tricky for me to articulate complex thoughts or big emotions, and sometimes, what comes out isn't quite right. Please be patient and give me time to find my words. If I'm struggling, offer me comfort and the chance to try again. Active listening is critical; it shows you're trying to understand, not just hear me. When you listen to what I'm trying to say, not just what I manage to express, you help me feel heard and valued. You teach me that communication is more than just words—it's also about trying to understand each other. With your guidance, I'll learn to share my thoughts and feelings more clearly. Acknowledge the effort behind my jumbled words; it encourages me to keep trying. Your attentive ear and sensitive approach reassure me that my voice matters, and with each conversation, I am learning the invaluable skill of expressing myself authentically and confidently.

Example:

Five-year-old Emma was upset. She sat on the kitchen floor, her small brow furrowed, surrounded by an array of crayons and torn paper. Her mother, Mara, knelt beside her, observing the scene.

"What's going on, sweetheart?" Mara asked gently, her voice free of judgment.

"I can't do it right!" Emma exclaimed, her words tumbling out amidst sniffles.

Mara didn't immediately swoop in to fix the torn paper or reassure her with empty platitudes. Instead, she stayed present, offering a comforting smile and a patient ear.

"Tell me about it," Mara encouraged, recognizing that Emma was grappling with frustration and disappointment.

Emma tried to explain, but her words were a mix of childlike expressions and emotions that didn't quite translate into the issue at hand. Mara listened, not interrupting or correcting her daughter's imperfect attempts at communication.

After a few moments of listening, Mara gently offered, "It sounds like you're upset because the picture didn't turn out how you wanted it to?"

Emma nodded vigorously, relieved her mother understood.

Mara continued to listen as Emma explained her picture didn't look like the one she had in her mind. Instead of immediately offering a solution, Mara validated her daughter's feelings, "It's okay to be upset when things don't work out the way we plan."

They talked through Emma's feelings, Mara encouraging her daughter to describe what she had hoped to create. Together, they found a way to express those ideas differently, with Mara guiding Emma to understand that mistakes were part of learning and creating.

By the end of the conversation, Emma was back at the table, a fresh piece of paper in front of her, crayons confidently moving as she tried again.

At this moment, Mara demonstrated patience and the importance of active listening, allowing Emma to grow in her ability to communicate and express herself clearly.

14

Lesson 13: "Don't Try My Honesty Too Much"

- Building trust and honesty.
- How fear can lead to dishonesty.

"**Foster Trust, Not Fear.**"

Please remember that my honesty is delicate. If I'm afraid of getting in trouble, I might hide the truth to avoid punishment. I want to be honest with you, but I need to know that I can trust you with my mistakes. When I'm reassured that it's safe to be truthful, even when I've done something wrong, I learn that honesty is valued over perfection. Fear can be a significant obstacle to honesty; I might not be as forthcoming if I'm scared of your reaction. Help me understand that honesty leads to understanding and forgiveness, not just consequences. Show me that our relationship is a safe space where I can be open and truthful. This way, you're not just telling me to be honest; you're showing me how, and that trust between us will grow stronger.

Example:

Twelve-year-old Joe stood in the living room; his eyes fixed on the carpet. In his hand, he held the remnants of a broken vase. His father stood across from him, his expression calm and concerned rather than angry.

"Joe, can you tell me what happened here?" Dad asked, his tone steady.

Joe hesitated his usual impulse to weave a protective tale, wrestling with the knowledge of his father's approach to honesty. He remembered the last time he had broken a glass. Instead of a harsh punishment, his father had discussed the importance of being careful and responsible for one's actions.

"I was trying to get my ball from the shelf, and I knocked the vase over," Joe admitted, bracing himself for a rebuke that didn't come.

Dad nodded, "Thank you for telling me the truth. I appreciate your honesty more than the vase. Let's clean this up together and think about what we can do to avoid such accidents in the future."

As they swept up the pieces, Dad talked about responsibility and care for other people's belongings. He didn't diminish the importance of the loss, nor did he ignore the action, but he focused on the value of honesty and the opportunity to learn from mistakes.

Joe felt a warmth of gratitude. He knew he would be more careful in the future, not out of fear of punishment but because he valued the trust and respect that flowed between him and his father.

LESSON 13: "DON'T TRY MY HONESTY TOO MUCH"

Dad's approach fostered an environment where Joe could be honest without undue fear of retribution, understanding that honesty was a critical component of trust and respect within their relationship.

15

Lesson 14: "Don't Be Inconsistent"

- Consistency in parenting and its role in creating a stable environment.

"**Crave Consistency, Need Stability**"

When you're not consistent, it's like trying to build a house on shifting sand for me. Rules and routines help me understand what to expect; they make my world feel safer and more stable. If the rules keep changing, I get confused and might act out, not because I want to be naughty but because I'm trying to understand my boundaries. Inconsistency can feel like a storm, where I'm left to guess how the wind blows today. It's vital for you to be my compass, reliable and steady so that I can navigate life's challenges with confidence. Consistent parenting shows me love through structure and guides me in learning right from wrong. It helps me to trust you and the world around me and teaches me self-discipline that I'll carry into adulthood. Your consistency is the foundation I need to build my life.

LESSON 14: "DON'T BE INCONSISTENT"

Example:

Imagine a scenario where 8-year-old Angela faces the complexities of inconsistent parenting:

Angela sat at the kitchen table; her homework spread out before her. It was Thursday, which usually meant pizza night, a tradition she looked forward to all week. But as the clock ticked closer to dinner time, her mother announced they'd have the chicken salad instead.

"But Mom, it's pizza night," Angela protested, her face a mixture of disappointment and confusion.

"I know, sweetie, but I changed my mind. We're having salad now," her mother replied casually, oblivious to the impact of the sudden change.

Mom shook Angela's little world. The inconsistency was a small ripple in an adult's eye but a tidal wave in hers. Last week, when she had forgotten to feed the dog on her designated day, her father had dismissed it, saying it was okay just this once. Yet the week before, her mother had enforced extra chores due to the same oversight.

Such irregularities were not limited to household routines. Her parents' reactions to her grades fluctuated wildly, too. One day, they celebrated a 'B' with cheers; the next, they met the same grade with frowns and lectures about trying harder.

This inconsistency left Angela unsure of where she stood. Rules seemed to be mere suggestions, fluctuating with her parents' moods. As a result, she began to test boundaries, not out of rebellion but out of a need for some kind of predictable structure.

The inconsistency of her parents was teaching her an unintended lesson: that reliability was negotiable, and that the world was an unpredictable place. Angela craved the stability of consistent rules and routines, not just for the comfort they brought but for the trust in their established environment, allowing her to grow and learn within a secure framework.

16

Lesson 15: "Don't Tell Me You Don't Like Me When I Make Mistakes"

- Unconditional love versus behavior approval.
- Separating the child's identity from their actions.

"**Separate Me from My Mistakes**"

Please remember, when I mess up, it doesn't mean I'm a bad kid. I must know you dislike what I did, not who I am. Your words are powerful; they can shape how I see myself. When you say you don't like me because of something I've done, it's like saying I am my mistake. But I'm learning and I'll make many mistakes along the way. It's how I realize what's right and wrong. I need you to show me that there's a difference between my actions and my worth. Teach me that my behavior can change, but my value as a person doesn't. Love me even when I slip up and guide me to improve. That's how I'll grow to understand that I am loved unconditionally and that my actions, good or bad, aren't the whole of who I am.

Example:

Imagine 5-year-old Lana excitedly drew on the living room wall with her crayons:

Lana, with crayons in hand, looked up at the colorful scribbles adorning the wall—a proud smile across her face. However, her joy quickly faded as she noticed her father's frown from across the room.

"Why do you do things like this, Lana? This is naughty behavior," her father said, his voice tinged with disappointment.

The little girl's heart sank, and her eyes brimmed with tears. The bright streaks on the wall suddenly seemed like evidence of her being 'bad,' and she felt a painful pang in her heart, believing that her father's love might be conditional on her being 'good.'

"I just wanted to make it pretty," Lana whimpered, her tiny voice quivering with the fear of losing her father's affection.

Her father took a deep breath, realizing the impact of his words. He sat down beside her, his tone now calm and composed.

"Lana, you are a wonderful girl, and I love you very much. It's okay to make mistakes, and it's important to express your creativity, but there are better ways to do it than drawing on the wall," he hugged her gently. "Let's clean this up together and then find some paper for your next masterpiece, okay?"

As they cleaned the wall together, Lana learned a valuable lesson. Her actions might sometimes be misguided, and while she might face consequences, they didn't make her any less loved or useful. Her father's guidance showed her that she was cherished unconditionally and that while her behavior might need correction, her inherent worth was unquestionable.

17

Lesson 16: "Don't Say My Worries and Fear Are Nonsense"

- Validation of children's feelings.
- The importance of empathy and support.

"**Acknowledge My Fears**"

When I come to you with my worries and fears, please don't dismiss them as silly. To me, they're as big and natural as anything you experience. Ignoring what scares me doesn't make the monsters under my bed disappear—it just teaches me to hide them from you. I need your empathy and reassurance, not a judgment that my feelings are nonsense. Your support is my shield; it helps me feel safe enough to face my fears. When you take the time to listen and understand, you show me that my feelings are important. This teaches me to trust my emotions and to come to you when I'm scared. By validating my worries, you're not just calming my current fears but building my confidence to conquer future ones, with or without your help. It's a foundation of trust and understanding I'll carry with me as I

LESSON 16: "DON'T SAY MY WORRIES AND FEAR ARE NONSENSE"

grow.

Example:

Ethan clutched his dinosaur plushie, his eyes tracing the eerie shapes that the moonlight cast upon his room's walls. "Dad," he murmured, a tremble in his voice, "the shadows are scaring me."

His dad, pausing his bedtime book reading, glanced briefly at the walls and chuckled. "Ethan, those are just shadows. They're nothing to be scared of. It's all in your head, buddy."

The light laughter did little to ease Ethan's racing heart; instead, the shadows loomed more prominent in his imagination, now mixed with the hurt of being brushed off.

Noticing Ethan's discomfort hadn't ebbed, his dad set the book aside and scooted closer, his tone softening. "Hey, let's figure this out together. What do you see in those shadows?" he asked, inviting Ethan to share his fears.

With his dad's gentle prompting, Ethan pointed out the shapes that unnerved him. Together, they made a game of finding funny and friendly figures instead of scary ones. "See, that one looks like a goofy elephant, doesn't it?" his dad suggested, tracing the outline with his finger.

The room was the same, the shadows unchanged, but with his dad's warmth and validation, Ethan's fear was transformed into a shared adventure. The night was no longer a canvas for monsters but a backdrop for their imagination. This exchange, filled with understanding and support, became a cornerstone in Ethan's young life, teaching him that his feelings were valid and that he was never alone in facing them.

18

Lesson 17: "Don't Try to Tell Me That You Are Perfect and Flawless"

- The power of vulnerability in parenting.
- The impact of parents admitting their mistakes.

"**Embrace Your Imperfections**"

It's crucial for me to see that you're not perfect and that you, too, make mistakes. When you pretend to be flawless, it sets an impossible standard for me to live up to. But when you admit your own slip-ups, do something powerful—it shows me that mistakes are part of being human and that it's okay to be imperfect. This openness fosters a sense of common ground between us; I learned that it's normal to falter and that these moments are growth opportunities. Your vulnerability teaches me to be compassionate towards myself and others when mistakes happen. Most importantly, when you're honest about your flaws, it helps me to accept my own. It assures me that love and respect are not conditional upon being perfect, and this is a lesson that will help me navigate through life with kindness and self-acceptance.

Example:

"Mom, why did you apologize to the cashier just now?" Sophie asked, her curious eyes fixed on her mother as they walked from the grocery store.

Her mother smiled gently, taking Sophie's hand in hers. "Well, I was a bit short with her when she made a mistake with our shopping. Everyone has tough moments, sweetheart, including me. I was wrong, so I apologized."

Sophie pondered this; her brow furrowed. "But adults don't make mistakes, do they? You always tell me what to do."

"Oh, we make plenty," her mother chuckled. "I make them all the time. It's important to admit when you're wrong. That's how we learn and grow. How will you learn if I can't show you how to accept and learn from mistakes?"

Sophie's grip tightened around her mother's hand, a sign of comfort and understanding. "So, it's okay if I'm not perfect?"

"Absolutely," her mother assured her, her eyes full of warmth. "Perfection isn't the goal; being brave enough to face our imperfections is. Remember, it's okay to be a work in progress. We all are."

Sophie's steps grew more confident as they continued their walk. Her mother's admission had not only lifted the weight of expectation but woven a deeper thread of trust and connection between them. That day, Sophie learned a valuable lesson that day—not about the infallibility of adults but about the grace of vulnerability and the strength found in

LESSON 17: "DON'T TRY TO TELL ME THAT YOU ARE PERFECT AND...

the honesty of imperfection.

19

Lesson 18: "Never Think That It Is Below Your Dignity to Apologize to Me"

- Apologizing and its effects on parent-child relationships.
- Respect and understanding through mutual apologies.

"**Apologies: A Bridge to Respect and Understanding**"

When you apologize to me, it does more than just mend a mistake; it teaches me the value of humility and respect. Your apology isn't about losing dignity but elevating our relationship, demonstrating that our bond is based on mutual respect and understanding. It reassures me that my feelings matter and that you're committed to making things right when they go wrong. This exchange of apologies isn't just about apologizing—it's about acknowledging each other's perspectives and emotions. It becomes a powerful lesson in empathy, showing me how to navigate relationships with care and responsibility. Your willingness to apologize also sets a strong example for me to follow, teaching me to take accountability for my actions and to approach others with the same respect. When you apologize, you're

LESSON 18: "NEVER THINK THAT IT IS BELOW YOUR DIGNITY TO...

not just correcting a mistake—you're guiding me toward becoming more thoughtful and compassionate.

Example:

Eight-year-old Marcus stood quietly; his eyes downcast as his mother knelt before him. She had raised her voice earlier when he had accidentally spilled juice on her important work papers. Now, she took a deep breath, ready to bridge the gap her stern words had created.

"Marcus, I'm sorry for yelling at you earlier," she said sincerely. "It wasn't right of me to get so upset over an accident. Can you forgive me?"

Marcus looked up, surprised. "You're sorry? But moms and dads don't say sorry to kids…"

"They do, Marcus," his mother replied gently. "Everyone makes mistakes, even moms and dads. And when we do, we need to apologize, just like we ask you to do. It's how we show respect and care about each other's feelings."

A small smile began to form on Marcus's face. "I forgive you, Mom. And I'm sorry for the spill."

His mother hugged him tightly, her heart swelling with pride and love. "Thank you, Marcus. That means a lot to me."

As they held each other, a new layer of trust settled around them. Marcus had not only learned that it was okay to make mistakes and that it was essential to acknowledge them, no matter who you are. It was a lesson that would shape his understanding of respect, humility, and the power of a simple apology for years.

20

Lesson 19: "Don't Forget How Fast I'm Growing Up"

- The rapid pace of childhood development.
- Keeping up with changing needs and abilities.

Embracing the Swift Current of Growth

Please don't lose sight of how quickly I'm changing and growing. It feels like only yesterday I needed help tying my shoes only yesterday, and now I'm learning to navigate the world more independently. With each passing day, my needs and abilities evolve, often faster than we both might expect. You need to recognize and adapt to this growth—not just in how you care for me but in how you understand and interact with me. As I develop, so too should your expectations and how you support me. Embrace my newfound skills, encourage my growing interests, and be ready to let go just a little more, even if it's bittersweet. By keeping pace with my rapid development, you help ensure that I don't outgrow the guidance and love I still very much need, even if it's in different ways than before.

LEARNING LESSONS FROM RAISING CHILDREN

Example:

Imagine a scene where a father watches his 10-year-old daughter, Ella, meticulously pack her backpack for a school trip. The night before, they disagreed about whether she was old enough to go on the trip without family members.

"Dad, did you see I've packed everything myself?" Ella asks, her eyes shining with pride.

Her father nods, marveling at her competence. "I did, honey. You're getting so organized."

Ella sits beside him, her demeanor serious. "Dad, you remember when I used to be scared of sleepovers? Now I'm ready for this. But yesterday, you still looked at me like I was that little girl who couldn't sleep without her nightlight."

Her father takes in her words, the realization washing over him. "You're right, Ella. I was so focused on keeping you safe that I almost forgot how capable you became."

Ella leans against his shoulder. "I'll always need you, just in different ways now."

He wraps an arm around her, his heart both heavy and light. "I understand. I'll try to keep up with you to support the amazing person you're becoming."

As Ella talks excitedly about the trip, her father listens intently, acknowledging not just the child she was but the young person she is becoming.

LESSON 19: "DON'T FORGET HOW FAST I'M GROWING UP"

It's a moment of transition for them both, recognizing the swift current of childhood growth.

21

Lesson 20: "Don't Forget That I Can't Grow Up Well Without Lots of Love and Kind Understanding"

- The foundational need for love in a child's development.
- Encouraging a nurturing environment for growth.

The Essence of Nurturing: Love and Understanding

Remember, I can't bloom into my best self without a steady shower of love and a nurturing climate of understanding. Love is the rich soil that roots my development deeply, giving me the strength to reach upwards confidently. Your kindness and empathy are essential to my growth like the sun and rain, essential to my growth. They teach me to love in return and to understand the world around me. Without these, I'm like a sapling struggling to grow in barren ground. So, as I navigate the twists and turns of growing up, let your love be my guide and your understanding my support. These are not just the trimmings of a happy childhood but the core necessities that will enable me to flourish. In a garden of love and understanding, I will grow well and wondrously.

Example:

In the small hours of the evening, Jacob, a curly-haired eight-year-old with a penchant for questions, sits cross-legged on the living room rug, a disassembled toy train before him. He looks up at his mother, frustration etched in his young features.

"Mom, why won't it work?" he implores, his voice tinged with the day's defeats.

His mother, kneeling beside him, offers a smile that carries the warmth of a hundred suns. "Let's figure it out together," she says, her tone a gentle breeze of encouragement.

As they work side by side, her patient guidance helps Jacob navigate through his small yet significant struggle. With every piece they fit together, his mother's love is the silent yet powerful force that fuels his resilience.

Finally, with a soft click, the last part snaps into place. Jacob's face illuminates with a triumphant glow, his eyes reflecting the profound lesson learned—not just of gears and mechanics, but of the boundless potential within him, unlocked by his mother's steadfast love and understanding.

"See, you did it!" she exclaims, her pride in his achievement clear as daylight.

Jacob beams, his earlier frustration forgotten like a dream upon waking. "I did, didn't I? Because you helped me."

As they embrace, it's clear that this moment is about more than just fixing a toy; it's a testament to the nurturing spirit of love and understanding that is vital for Jacob to thrive. In this nurturing environment, Jacob is not just growing; he is blossoming into the person he is meant to be.

22

PARENTING INSIGHTS: KITCHEN WALL SUMMARY

"**DON'T SPOIL ME.**"
I know well that I shouldn't get everything I want. I'm just testing you.
"**DO NOT BE AFRAID TO BE STRICT AND STRONG.**"
I like it - I feel safer that way.
"**DON'T LET ME CREATE BAD HABITS.**"
I have to rely on you that you will reveal them.
"**DON'T TREAT ME YOUNGER THAN I ACTUALLY AM.**"
It makes me act silly when I get older.
"**DON'T SCOLD ME, PUNISH ME, OR REPRIMAND ME IN PUBLIC.**"
I am far more impressed when you talk to me peacefully and privately.
"**DON'T FORCE ON ME THAT MY MISTAKES ARE MORTAL SINS.**"
It destroys my sense of values.
"**DON'T BE TOO MAD WHEN I SAY I HATE YOU.**"
It is not you that I don't like, but your power that threatens me.
"**DO NOT PROTECT ME FROM ALL THE CONSEQUENCES**

OF MY ACTIONS."

I need to learn to bear hardships and pain.

"DON'T PAY EXCESSIVE ATTENTION TO MY MINOR INJURIES."

I can handle them.

"DON'T SCOLD ME."

I would have to defend myself by being deaf and pretending to be a dead bug.

"DON'T MAKE HASTY PROMISES."

Remember, I feel disappointed when you don't keep them.

"REMEMBER THAT I CANNOT ALWAYS EXPRESS MYSELF AS CLEARLY I WANT TO."

That's why I'm sometimes not entirely precise, and I can't be understood.

"DON'T TRY MY HONESTY TOO MUCH."

I get scared, and then I lie.

"DON'T BE INCONSISTENT."

That confuses me.

"DON'T TELL ME YOU DON'T LIKE ME WHEN I MAKE MISTAKES."

"DON'T SAY MY WORRIES AND FEARS ARE NONSENSE."

For me, they seem extremely real and it means the world to me when you try to understand.

"DON'T TRY TO TELL ME THAT YOU ARE PERFECT AND FLAWLESS."

It really upsets me when I find out that it's not like that.

"NEVER THINK THAT IT IS BELOW YOUR DIGNITY TO APOLOGIZE TO ME."

After a sincere apology, my relationship with you becomes even warmer.

"DON'T FORGET HOW FAST I'M GROWING UP."

It's definitely hard to keep up with me, but please - try!

"DON'T FORGET THAT I CAN'T GROW UP WELL WITHOUT

LOTS OF LOVE AND KIND UNDERSTANDING."
I don't have to tell you that, do I?

23

Conclusion

Understanding the Heart of Parenting: A Child's Perspective

Across the canvas of childhood, the twenty messages we've explored paint a vivid picture of the delicate balance required in nurturing a child. From the pitfalls of overindulgence to the importance of honesty, consistency, and unconditional love, each message underscores a facet of the complex gem of the parent-child relationship. They remind us that discipline should be a guide, not a punishment, and that mistakes are stepping stones to learning, not weights that drown us in guilt.

The overarching narrative woven through these messages is straightforward: children thrive in environments where understanding, empathy, and love are the cornerstones. It's not enough to provide for a child's physical needs; their emotional and psychological landscapes are equally crucial. Every "I hate you" has a more profound yearning for connection, every fear a plea for reassurance, and every act of defiance a test of boundaries.

Parents are encouraged to look beyond the surface to hear the unspoken needs

CONCLUSION

that children may struggle to articulate. It's in the silent moments, the shared glances, and the pauses between words that much is said. Parents can foster an atmosphere where children feel heard, valued, and loved by listening to both the said and the unsaid.

This journey of understanding is not one-sided. As parents display their humanity, admit their flaws, and embrace the vulnerability of apologizing, they model the very behaviors they wish to instill in their children. This mutual growth cultivates a relationship built on respect, trust, and empathy.

Effective communication between children and parents is pivotal for a healthy, nurturing relationship. It encompasses words and a holistic exchange of feelings, needs, and mutual understanding. From birth, children communicate through cries and looks, evolving to words and complex expressions as they grow. Parents must guide them in refining their language and empathetic communication.

Understanding a child's message is often challenging, as they may lack the vocabulary or emotional maturity to be precise. Misbehavior might be a cry for attention rather than simple defiance; a quiet mood could indicate more profound issues. Parents need to decode these signals, listening actively and responding with empathy.

This nuanced understanding shapes parenting actions and responses, distinguishing when to discipline and when to offer support. It establishes trust and openness, encouraging children to share openly without fear of judgment. Parents' sensitive responses to their children's emotional states also foster emotional intelligence, teaching children to express and manage their emotions effectively, laying the groundwork for social resilience and competence.

LEARNING LESSONS FROM RAISING CHILDREN

In conclusion, these twenty messages serve as a compass for parents, guiding them toward the nurturing warmth every child requires. Children learn to navigate the complexities of emotions and relationships through understanding and empathy. And through love, they find the strength to grow into compassionate, resilient individuals. Let these messages remind us that in the world of a child, the greatest gift a parent can give is their heart's attentive presence, guiding them through life's tapestry with a steady, loving hand.

24

THANK YOU!

If this book has enriched your experience, I would be deeply grateful if you could spare a moment to leave a positive review on Amazon. Your feedback is rewarding and reaffirms the purpose of my writing and sharing knowledge. Thank you for making my day brighter with your support.

Simply scan the QR code below, click the rating,
scroll down and leave your review:

www.ingramcontent.com/pod-product-compliance
Lightning Source LLC
Chambersburg PA
CBHW050247010526
44107CB00003B/215